The Play

by Gloria Rose

illustrated by
Luciana Navarro Alves

Editorial Offices: Glenview, Illinois • Parsippany, New Jersey • New York, New York
Sales Offices: Needham, Massachusetts • Duluth, Georgia • Glenview, Illinois
Coppell, Texas • Sacramento, California • Mesa, Arizona

Illustrations by Luciana Navarro Alves

ISBN: 0-328-13163-6

4 5 6 7 8 9 10 V010 14 13 12 11 10 09 08 07 06

What could the class do?

The class will put on a play.

What could Kate do?

Kate will be a yellow bird.

What could Grace and Jake do?

Grace and Jake will make

a horse from old paper.

What could Nate do?
Nate will make trees
for the stage.

What could the class do?

The class will put on the play.

Putting on a Play!

Many people work together to put on a play. One person is the director. The director tells the actors what to do. Other people make costumes. Others make and paint the scenery. Some helpers turn the stage lights on and off or play music.